Angel! Angel!
What Do You See?

Written by Cherie Pless Dittmer
Illustrated by Lauren Gallegos

CONCORDIA PUBLISHING HOUSE · SAINT LOUIS

Concordia
Publishing House

Founded in 1869 as the publishing arm of The Lutheran
Church—Missouri Synod, Concordia Publishing House gives
all glory to God for the blessing of 150 years of opportunities
to provide resources that are faithful to the Holy Scriptures
and the Lutheran Confessions.

Published by Concordia Publishing House
3558 S. Jefferson Avenue, St. Louis, MO 63118-3968
1-800-325-3040 • cph.org
Text © 2002 Cherie Pless Dittmer
Artwork © 2019 Concordia Publishing House

Scripture quotation is from the ESV® Bible (The Holy Bible, English Standard
Version®), copyright © 2001 by Crossway, a publishing ministry of Good News
Publishers. Used by permission. All rights reserved.
Manufactured in Shenzhen, China/055760/330252

1 2 3 4 5 6 7 8 9 10   28 27 26 25 24 23 22 21 20 19

To my children, Emily, Anna, Erin, Abigail, and Jonathan, with whom I love to share Christmas joys and laughter!

This book is also dedicated to all who interact with young children. Read and enjoy this rhythmic telling of our Savior's birth. Allow the children the creative freedom to celebrate this story of God's grace in song, dance, and drama. One reading of this storybook and the children will be eager to say it and sing it and tell it to others.

A joyful Christmas sharing will happen!

Angel! Angel!
what do you see?

I see Mary
will have a baby!

Mary! Mary!
what do you see?

I see a donkey
carrying me.

Donkey! Donkey!

What do you see?

I see Joseph
gently leading me.

Joseph! Joseph!

What do you see?

I see an innkeeper
welcoming me.

Innkeeper!
Innkeeper!

What do you see?

I see a spotted cow
mooing softly.

Spotted cow!
Spotted cow!

What do you see?

I see a woolly sheep,
soft and cuddly.

Woolly Sheep!
Woolly Sheep!

What do you see?

I see a shepherd
carrying me.

Shepherd! Shepherd!

What do you see?

I see the angels
singing to me.

Angels! Angels!

What do you see?

We see a new star
shining brightly.

Bright Star! Bright Star!

What do you see?

I see the Wise Men
following me.

Wise Man!
Wise Man!

What do you see?

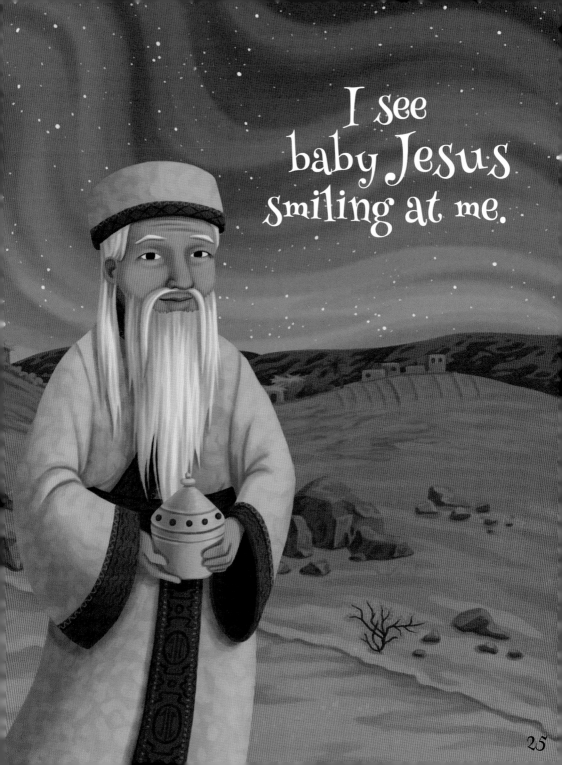

I see
baby Jesus
smiling at me.

25

Baby Jesus! Baby Jesus!

What do You see?

I see God's children
loving Me!

God's Child! God's Child!

what do YOU see?

I see my Savior, who
gave His life for me!

For God so loved
the world, that
He gave His only Son,
that whoever believes in Him
should not perish but have eternal life.

John 3:16